a bouquet of daisies

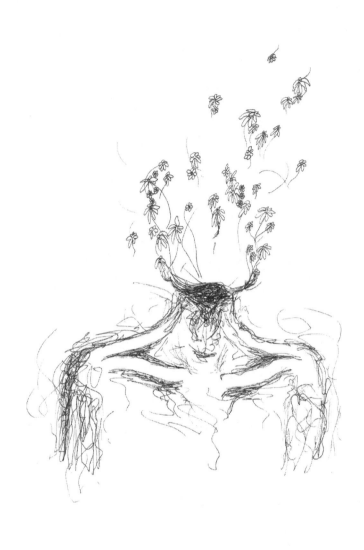

A BOUQUET
of daisies

POEMS

Megan Alice

GREEN WRITERS PRESS   Brattleboro, Vermont

Printed in the United States

10 9 8 7 6 5 4 3 2 1

Green Writers Press is a Vermont-based publisher whose mission is to spread a message of hope and renewal through the words and images we publish. Throughout we will adhere to our commitment to preserving and protecting the natural resources of the earth. To that end, a percentage of our proceeds will be donated to environmental activist groups. In addition, the poet will make a donation to Planned Parenthood Federation from her proceeds. Green Writers Press gratefully acknowledges support from individual donors, friends, and readers to help support the environment and our publishing initiative.

GReen
wriTers
press

Giving Voice to Writers & Artists Who Will Make the World a Better Place
Green Writers Press | Brattleboro, Vermont
www.greenwriterspress.com

ISBN: 978-1-7320815-6-7

COVER ART: Kira Hirsch

Women's Business Enterprise
National Council
WBEN℀

FSC

PRINTED ON PAPER WITH PULP THAT COMES FROM FSC-CERTIFIED FORESTS, MANAGED FORESTS THAT
GUARANTEE RESPONSIBLE ENVIRONMENTAL, SOCIAL, AND ECONOMIC PRACTICES BY McNAUGHTON & GUNN,
A WOMAN-OWNED BUSINESS CERTIFIED BY THE WOMEN'S BUSINESS ENTERPRISE NATIONAL COUNCIL.

Sometimes you make choices in life and sometimes choices make you.

—GAYLE FORMAN

For my dad. I love you.

CONTENTS

LOVE

ROSES: PART I

If you and I were roses,
You would stumble into love for my petals and perfume
I would dive into love for your roots and thorns

ROSES: PART II

My petals and size
my stalk standing straight
the symmetry of my leaves

Your roots and thorns
your lack of petals
the chewed-off edges of your leaves

If you and I were roses

ON YOUR SKIN AND MINE

If I could
I would write melodies
and
harmonies
and
poems with words so divine
I would write
sonnets
and
soliloquies
and
monologues
and all that came to mind
I would write these
for you
with only my lips
on your skin and mine

FIRST LOVE

Do you remember that day
you spun me around the kitchen
dancing like a drunken fool
I smiled and said,
"My ribs are broken in two, and I blame you."
You hushed, "Why is that?"
"You make me laugh too much."

Now I think
you made me love you too much.

HER

If souls could turn to energy
she would light every inch of Paris
and I think fate designed the crumbs of her soul
to line along the seam of mine
so that together
we could light every inch of the sun

YOU ARE MY FAVORITE POEM

Poetry is my voice and vice
the way I make sense of myself, of this world,
is through words.
But when you look at me,
my lips dry and my tongue weakens.
I lose all poetry in your presence.
My position as poet is instantly revoked.
I could never write anything as beautiful as you.

NEVER

He's never called me beautiful
the words
lovely
intricate
confident
drip from his lips
and that
is so much more sincere
and that
is what makes him a man

FLAWS & FLOWERS

Broken flowers are my favorite
the way their fragile bodies stand
compelling me to kneel and touch and linger longer
someday the seeds will fall to grow back stronger

You remind me of a broken flower
hands like silky petals of a rose against bare skin
aroma on your tattered jean jacket, covered in raindrops
voice slips vowels as morning dewdrops slip off rooftops

Snow White's lips were as red as blood
at least that's what the brothers claim
your lips are cracked and pale but taste of mint
then again you tend to pull back before I can leave
     an imprint

You fill up my senses!
That song would spill over my stereo all night
my love, you overflow my senses, it is true, you do
I love broken flowers as much as I love the broken parts
     of you

REAL

I knew it was real
when you kissed my temple
your fingertips grazed my hair,
tucked the loose strands behind my ear
I was awake
you thought I was asleep

HURT

Saturday Trespassing

Down the street from the place I should call home
An abandoned mansion sits above an orange grove
Glass front door framed with sleek iron but bordered up
    with wood
Vines of unkempt bougainvillea squeeze the half-painted
    walls
Tiles to be put on the roof lay in a cluttered heap by the
    garage doors
Piled on top of each other like children immersed in a tickle
    fight
Switches for the outside lights have been pulled out of their
    sockets
Dead leaves bury the pavement,
beer bottles poke their heads out of the dirt

On Saturdays, I sit on the steps to watch the day go by

My thoughts come and go like clouds,
shifting every few seconds until they're out of view
Sometimes I like to imagine what Gatsby might have done
    with the place
Which famous paintings would he choose to hang along the
    hallways?
Other times I try picturing a family living here
Toddlers running around the poolside,
their legs too chubby to go the speed they want

But the game never lasts long, and the clouds drift back to
   me, this time full of rain

And rather than turn the faucet of my tangled thoughts off I
   let the water overflow me
And suddenly none of these Saturday trespassings are about
   getting away from home
But getting away from myself

"HAPPY GIRLS ARE THE PRETTIEST."

The corners of her mouth pull back like show
curtains to
reveal a smile so grand, so perfectly rehearsed.
Boys in the audience subconsciously begin
drooling over her lips.
Soon, she knows, applause will fill the air.
If she's lucky, a pool of roses will gather at her feet.

I observe from the balcony.
I watch her jaw clench, her eyes shift side to
side. I end up crying.
Crying because I know, crying because I've
been her before.

If they knew her smile wasn't anyhing but an
exhausting play.
I know their *love* for her would never stay.

MAJOR DEPRESSIVE DISORDER

When I'm crying on my cracked bathroom tile
over nothing but my own mind they say I'm too
dramatic, or
that I only need to be more positive.
They tell me, "It's your own fault, you never
get out of bed!"
or, "You really shouldn't be this focused on
yourself!"
For the love of God, stop asking me if I've tried
drinking chamomile tea before bed as if I
should wake with my entire brain chemistry
rearranged correctly like it is that easy.
If I could conjure myself a cure, I would. So
please,
stop treating my illness like it is an angsty
phase of my behavior

YOU AREN'T YOU

Sure, I'd fuck her.
How do these words slither their way in
between your teeth?
Are those lips the same lips that met mine?
How can this be the same you
who asked me to dance in the kitchen at
midnight,
or who would place daisies in my hair while we
walked?
Love, I do not know you, not anymore.
But God do I ache for you.

THRONE

I used to hate that house
The towering ceilings made me insignificant
The cheap carpet of my bedroom made my skin itch
And the iron chandeliers looked like lifeless black widows

Every room overflowed with color and daylight
All but my dad's mahogany walled office
He kept the tapestries closed to swallow the sun
His desk clear except for a laptop and a single pen

Knick Knacks like an engine room telegraph stood on the
    shelves in back
Draped curtains swallowed all sunlight
A royal blue chair stood in the corner to face the tapestries
Gold buttons speckling the armrests

The chair enveloped my dainty twelve-year-old body

There were some slashes and holes in the leather; made by
    my younger self
To anyone else, it was a vintage piece of useless furniture

To me, it was my throne

When I wanted to be in a place where silence would take
over me
When I was told godfather had three months left to live
When I saw mama cry for the first time, her body violently
shaking
I fled to my throne to watch the rain crawl down the
window sill instead

Multiple times mama came to find me asleep on my throne
instead of my room

She scolded me saying it was daddy's workroom—not mine
I stared at the uneven tile floor when she said this
She knew as well as I did, daddy wasn't coming home until
he had to

1:28 AM

I wish the roof of my bedroom would swing open
I could sit and stare as the stars pooled in with haste
wrap me up in constellations
I would have pacified conversations with the man on the
    moon
tell him how lonely I convince myself to be
maybe he would laugh
tell me I know nothing
say through the slur of his lips
"I have no one. You have everyone."
and I would nod with a shy smile
knowing he is wise and I should listen
but pain suffocates the heart differently on everyone
so perhaps I am as lonely as my planetary friend
but we feel it both in different ways
you see, he truly has no one
while I have seven billion
seven billion souls who all have no idea
what it is like to be me
and that gut feeling is just as lonely
as having no one at all

FELT LESS

I've been staring at this blank page for an hour,
trying to force my pen in hand to cooperate.
Emotions have found a way to slip through my seems.
I would rather be heaving hot tears and
have them sear down my cheeks,
than sit here counting cracks in the ceiling—wondering
     when
I will feel human again

"DON'T BE SUCH A FEMINIST."

Today I was told, "don't be such a feminist,"
by a classmate I have known for five years.
I tell him that I wouldn't be a feminist if I
didn't have to be.
In my childhood home, a poster hung on the
bathroom wall.
It read, "In the garden of people, daughters are
the roses."
As a child, I thought that meant I was special
and wanted.
I went to school believing I was a rose but boys
treated me
like gum stuck under someone's desk, bound to
get caught in someone else's sticky fingers. I
wouldn't have to be a feminist if we lived in a
world where I could walk to my car at night
without staring at the sidewalk, checking to see
if someone's silhouette blankets over mine. I
wouldn't have to be a feminist if one in three
women weren't sexually assaulted before the
age of 18. I wouldn't have to be a feminist if
37% of transgender women weren't sexually
assaulted at one point in their lifetime, or if
American Indian women weren't two times
more likely to experience sexual assault than
any other race.

I wouldn't have to be a feminist if women
weren't shoved into cardboard boxes and
thrown into the attic like rag dolls.
Women are humans, not play toys. We are
flesh, blood, muscle, and trillions of cells. I will
stop being "such a feminist" when women of
every walk of life are treated and welcomed as
equals. I don't care what it takes because I don't
know if I'll ever have a daughter. Not if I have
to watch the life drain out of her eyes as she
says the words,
"Me too, mom."

IN A WORLD OF MY OWN

In a world of my own
beauty is the only tragedy one cries for and
living is not a forsaken reminder

In a world of my own
youth is held onto even in death and
love is artwork full of bliss

Everything would be what it isn't
in a world of my own

ONE SIDED LOVE LETTER

I ache for you in a way that nearly kills me
(why is it you never ask to see me?)
I memorize the novels that float out of your mouth like
    music notes
(please stop interrupting me)
If I asked, would you write me a love letter so loud my name
    echoes off its walls?

(the last letter you wrote me took up half a page)
(why don't you pour yourself over the page like I do?)
I have graffitied the walls of thousands of letters with your
    name
(the ones I can't bring myself to send are stuck in my
    drawer)
I can't help but think and think and think and think
maybe this is a one-sided love letter

and you are here for the thrill of receiving mail

IT'S BEEN A YEAR SINCE I'VE HEARD YOUR VOICE

You sang me ballads without speaking
cradled me to sleep without touch
lying there next to you
breathing out of sync
watching your eyelashes dance
I would give anything
to fall asleep that way
to be in love that way
one last time

BURNING

They say I've got fire in me like it's a good thing,
like I want to be curled up in this hate
my fire is deep anger, fueled by the flames of a memory—
I was eleven and kneeling by my bedside,
asking God for a new body because the one
I had didn't feel mine anymore.

God didn't answer, he left me to burn
started as a flicker, melted me away like a candlestick
now I can't have anyone's hands on me without thinking it's
    him, it's him and suddenly I want to rip off every layer
    of flesh until I'm nothing but a long ribbon of nerves
    because
they all, all of them, feel exactly like him.

He's an ocean away but the flames lick my mind like a shock
    collar, and then I'm back: my dress, the hallway, his shoes,

the peeled off paint in the corner, the whole scene is played
    out
flames spread from mind to body, I am burning alive
watching myself melt away, yes I am furious
but I'm mostly petrified.

There's no amount of water to flush out my fire
or at least none that I can find

I will have to extinguish these flames myself
my mind is scorching, my skin like paper, but I know
one day the flames of that memory and him will be nothing
    to me
nothing but a faint smell of smoke

MANIPULATION

PUPPETEER

You've got me wound around your wrists
strings fighting to hold me up
my arms droop above my hanging head, knees turned in
make sure I look happy!
make sure my cries stay muted!
I do not want to reach up and cut ties
but if I don't I will lose my mind,
and I would so much rather
lose you

DRIVE

You drove away
in that stupid sports car
and I cried
and cried
and cried
as my legs gave out from underneath me
you never said goodbye
not a word
or kiss
and the worst part is
I know you did it
on purpose

ART THIEF

You cut me apart
piece by piece
to rearrange me
the way you wanted
so now I am
a puzzle showing no picture
a canvas of mashed paint
and it would be easier to place
the blame and hatred against you
but really this was my mistake.
I know better than to fall for the ones
who pluck budding flowers
from their innocent beds
only to gaze later and
wonder
why
they
died.

CANCER

You are a leech full of cancer
you bubble my blood with insects
pump my brain with bleach
don't you see?
flowers shrivel when you walk by
venom dribbles from your curved lips
my heart is slowing
a machine without oil
my organs rot
veins snap in half
and soon enough
I won't have a voice
to tell you how much
you
are
killing
me

ALL I AM

A hand to reach when the lights go off

a voice to slice the silence when you cannot find your words
my love, you do not need
or want me at all
you crave the fleeting moments
when I can feed your famine for affection
or peel depression's shadow off your back
that is all I am to you
no matter how badly I want to be more

INTO NOTHING

Heart enveloped in chains
keys lost to the pit of my stomach
an indestructible knight
a goddess of avoiding pain
and like any great kingdom
centuries were spent in agony to construct my empire
but then you came and in six seconds

you unraveled
my nerves
and cells
and veins
and chains
to turn me into nothing but
grains of sand slipping
through an hourglass

VITULA

My heart has strings strung taut across it
a lovely violin
and when I met you
you promised me you wouldn't play
no matter how much you adored making music
I smiled
and believed you
then I dozed off
so you placed my heart underneath your chin
and broke off a piece of my rib for a bow
minutes became hours as hours became weeks
until my heartstrings snapped from being wound much
 too tight

and when my eyes shot open from the splitting whiplash
I saw you frown
and walk away
what once was a magnificent instrument
is now just
a muscle
doing its job pumping oxygen

OUT DAMNED YOU

Traces of you run up and down along my skin. Lines
crisscrossing like highways over, under, and in between the
    seems

like a permanent ink only I can see. I spend nights
drawn over into morning scrubbing you away,
down on my hands and knees with washcloths.
Rubbing my skin raw to erase the taint of you.
In the morning I douse myself in sweet-smelling perfumes

to mask your musky scent that seizes my nose
like a leech latches onto wet flesh.
For you are everywhere and nowhere all at once
and I have been drowning in you since I met you.

HAD A BAD DREAM WITH MY EYES OPEN

you want me the way a toddler
collects rocks to shove in a mason jar
or fills a box with stuffed animals to place in the attic
you want me the way a child keeps their toys
locked away underneath the bed next to monsters
you only want me when you're bored
and it takes a radically messed up soul
to think a woman can be treated like a ragdoll
and what a plot twist it is
when the only monster
is the one sleeping under the sheets

SELF CARE IS NOT SELFISH

We sit on the carpet cross-legged,

picking up splintered pieces of
each other from the floor to place in the right spot.
All I want is to piece you back together, I want you
to see yourself as something whole, something more than
    hurting.
I am not leaving because there are more fractured pieces
    than I
bargained for, but because you are a puzzle I cannot rack
    my brain to
 solve, and taking the time to glue you back together
only shatters me further.

HEALING

NIGHTTIME REMINDER

Sometimes
that memory of you
crawls its way out of the cobwebs
and more than anything, I want to
plunge my nails into my lips
peel off the pink stained skin
and kill the taste of you
but I don't
because I know
destroying my body
will not destroy your haunting

PLATONIC BREAKUP

I met eyes with an old friend
in a cafe on the outskirts of the city
her face fell into a conjure of confused melancholy.
She was reacting to my situation.
The poetry book, the teacup, the empty opposite side of the
        booth—as if this scene was precisely what she feared she
had left me with. As if the act of spending time alone
for yourself is a sure sign of necessary therapy.
Please don't think I am sitting here in this coffee shop
brooding over what we used to be. Maybe I loved the
        security of your
returning adoration for me at one time, but I do not miss the
        way we
convinced ourselves we needed each other.

Not anymore.

HOLLOW BODY

I stood there alone
underneath the glass sky
watched with dry eyes
emptied your hollow body into damp soil
I had to shovel you out of my mind
get your crawling skin six feet deep from mine
it killed every ounce of me to do this
but I did it
because I had to
I had to
so please, let me learn to be myself again
and for God's sake
do not make me bury you
again

BOTH

I am an exploding sun
and
an infinite tunnel
I am a fire swallowing forests whole
and
I am a flood without an ark
do not love me for my light
and
expect to never
be encased in dark

SATURDAY

There is something so seductive about
cars and music and windows down.
Something so intimate about being alone with the wind
something about it quiets my nervous system as if the wind
    curls around my neck like a fur coat to stop my mind
    from racing.

At least for a little while.
Something about it induces me to sing against the lump of
    pain sludged in my throat
like honey that seeps through cracks of burnt toast

My tears fall easy
but not on Saturday

MY LIFE NEEDS TO BE REWRITTEN

Too often
I find myself loving with nothing but
quotation marks and asterisks
shouldn't I love with nothing but exclamation points and the
    occasional bracket for our secrets?
Too often
I find myself living with nothing but
periods at the end of the day, begging tomorrow to start
Shouldn't I be living with nothing but commas?
and the more pressing question is:
if I'm not living with commas or loving with exclamation
    points
am I living or loving at all?

WAS

I often wonder
how much of myself
I could be if I stopped
carrying around the luggage
of who I was and who I should be
and would I even recognize her?

A BOUQUET OF DAISIES

Rolling over onto my side,
my ear catches the melody of the rain kissing the roof,
causing my mind to wander over to mama's rose garden.
The image of her roses tipping their heads to soak in
    mouthfuls of water
calms me down before anxiety has a chance to reach me.

With my eyes closed and the right amount of silence present,
I can focus on the music of the soft orchestra happening
    beyond me.
Bliss takes over me when I realize I can hear everything.
    Everything. A
part of me is convinced I can hear mama's roses begin to
    bloom.
I want to see if I'm right.

For a second,
I let my eyes flutter until they lose their heaviness.
Extending my hand to pull back my curtains I let my eyes
    adjust to the
blue hue of morning. Sure enough,
Mama's roses are tipping their heads to the heavens.

Slumping back into my pillow I catch a glimpse of white.
    There, on my
nightstand, a bouquet of daisies freshly picked rest gracefully
    in a
teapot. My heart swells. What seems like a feeling from eons
    ago, a
feeling only a portion of me has known before,
I am okay.

avec tout mon coeur,

Meryflice

Acknowledgements

To my mom - Someday, I hope to be at least half the woman you are. Nothing makes me more proud than being your daughter. Thank you for believing in me, taking care of me, and teaching me what it means to be a woman. I love you. Endlessly.

To my sisters - I don't know who I would be without you two. Being stuck with you for the rest of my life is a blessing. Thank you for loving me unconditionally. I admire both of you beyond words. I love you.

To Dede – Thank you for being such a warm human being. You have made this process everything I could have ever wanted it to be and more. I can't thank you enough. You believed in me when I didn't.

To Tami – This book is because of you. Four years ago I never would have thought that I would be an author. You built my confidence and my imagination. I am so grateful for you.

To Laura – This book would also not be possible without you. Thank you for supporting me and my writing. You are such an incredible woman! I look up to you as a role model in every way.

To Adria – You know how much you mean to me. Thank you for listening to me and being one of the few people who can really hear me when I speak.

To my readers – Thank you. Especially if you've read all the way to here! I love you! Thank you! I hope you leave this book feeling a bit more healed.